WHO WAS DWIGHT D. EISENHOWER?

Biography of US Presidents

Children's Biography Books

Speedy Publishing LLC
40 E. Main St. #1156
Newark, DE 19711
www.speedypublishing.com
Copyright 2017

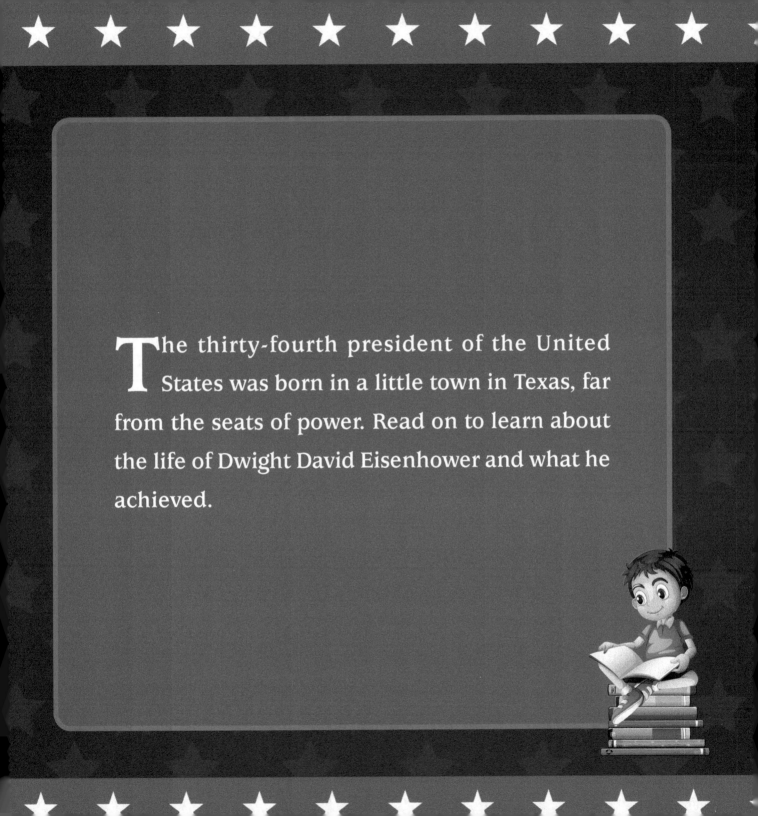

The thirty-fourth president of the United States was born in a little town in Texas, far from the seats of power. Read on to learn about the life of Dwight David Eisenhower and what he achieved.

EARLY LIFE

Dwight David Eisenhower was born in 1890 in Texas, and grew up in Kansas. His family was not well off and it was a struggle to raise a family of seven brothers. From when he was small he was known as "Ike".

FAMILY HOUSE

Eisenhower's mother was strongly opposed to the use of military force. He applied to enter the United States Military Academy anyhow, and was accepted to the course at West Point, New York. He graduated from West Point in 1915 and was posted to a base in Texas as a second lieutenant. There he met Mamie Doud, and they married in 1916. They had two children, one of whom died young.

A MILITARY MAN

The countries of Europe had been at war since 1914, and the United States entered the war on 1917 on the side of Great Britain and France against Germany. Ike was supposed to join an army unit there, but the war ended in 1918 before his orders came through.

GENERAL JOHN PERSHING

In peacetime Eisenhower studied at the Command and General Staff College in Kansas, and graduated at the top of his class. He became an aide to General John Pershing, who had commanded the U.S. ground forces in World War I.

Later, Ike transferred to the staff of General Douglas MacArthur, Chief of Staff of the Army. From 1935 to 1939 Eisenhower was on duty in the Philippines as a Lieutenant Colonel.

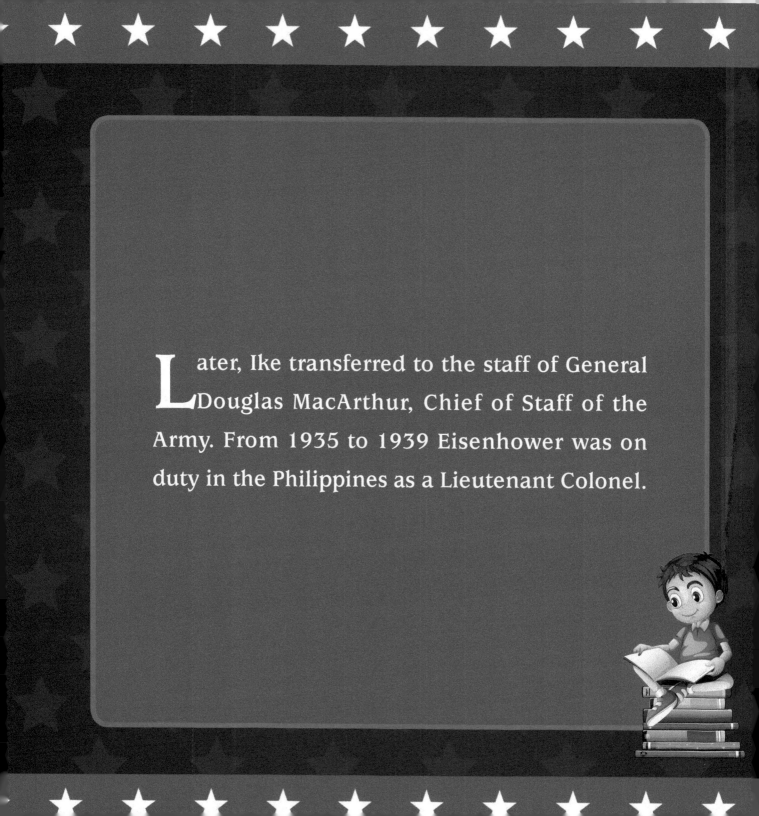

GENERAL DOUGLAS MACARTHUR

WORLD WAR II - POLAND

WORLD WAR II

When Germany invaded Poland in 1939 and other countries came to Poland's defense, a new war broke out in Europe. Read Baby Professor books like The Allied Powers vs. the Axis Powers in World War II and The Theaters of World War II: Europe and the Pacific to learn more about this war, which raged around the world from 1939 to 1945.

Eisenhower became a General in September, 1941. In December, after Japan attacked the U.S. fleet at Pearl Harbor in Hawaii, Eisenhower joined the military planning office in Washington, DC. He reported to General George Marshall, the Army Chief of Staff.

Ike was put in charge of Operation Torch, the invasion of North Africa by U.S. and allied troops, in 1942. This effort combined with British advances west from Egypt to surround and collapse Axis forces in North Africa.

After the German surrender in North Africa, Eisenhower was in charge of the invasion of Sicily and mainland Italy in 1943. Italian, and then German troops fought back hard and every foot of territory was contested, but by June of 1944 the Allies had liberated the Italian capital, Rome, and Italy was out of the war.

INVASION OF SICILY

INVASION OF NORMANDY

Based on the success of the invasion of Italy, Eisenhower became the commander of the Allied Expeditionary Force that would invade the rest of Nazi-occupied western Europe. The plans were complex, and include deceptions and even entire imaginary army units (with tanks made of cardboard and netting) to fool German spies and aerial observers. Finally, in June, 1944, over 150,000 Allied troops came ashore in Normandy, France, and started the process of pushing through and surrounding the German occupiers.

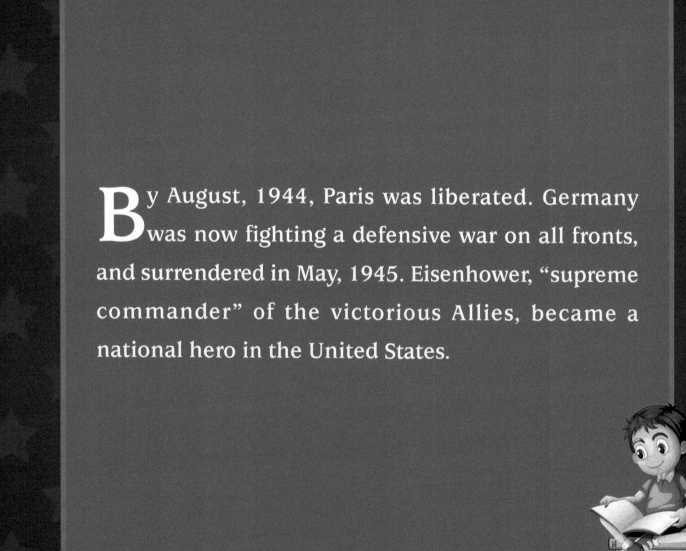

By August, 1944, Paris was liberated. Germany was now fighting a defensive war on all fronts, and surrendered in May, 1945. Eisenhower, "supreme commander" of the victorious Allies, became a national hero in the United States.

GENERAL DWIGHT D. EISENHOWER

WORLD WAR I

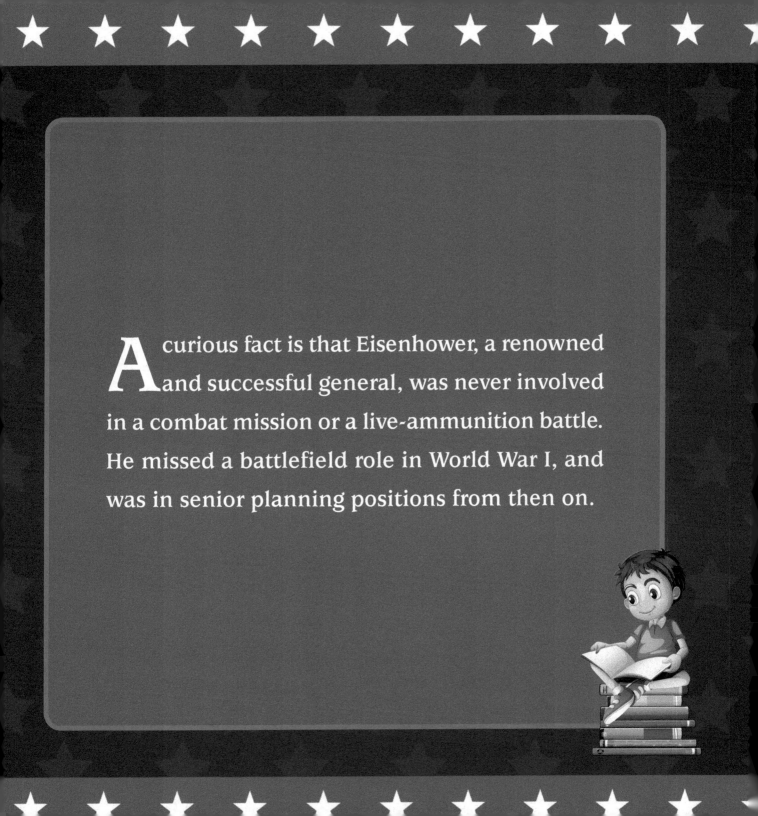

A curious fact is that Eisenhower, a renowned and successful general, was never involved in a combat mission or a live-ammunition battle. He missed a battlefield role in World War I, and was in senior planning positions from then on.

COLUMBIA UNIVERSITY

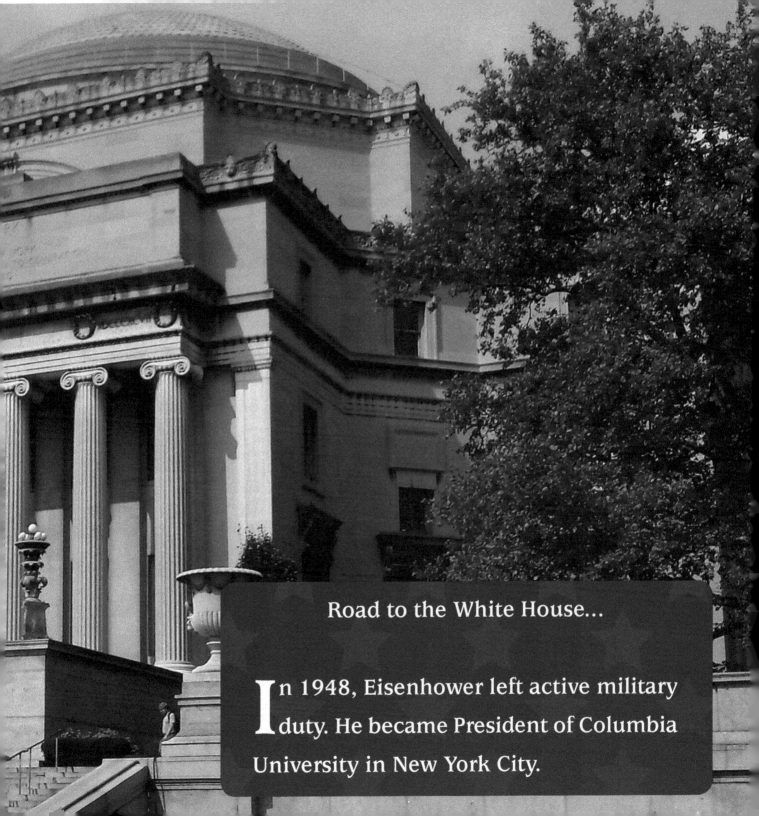

Road to the White House...

In 1948, Eisenhower left active military duty. He became President of Columbia University in New York City.

PRESIDENT HARRY S. TRUMAN

However, President Harry Truman asked Eisenhower to return to active duty in 1950. He became head of the military forces in Europe of a new organization, the North Atlantic Treaty Organization (NATO). Eisenhower helped develop the command structure and systems right down to the resupply of troops that would let forces from many countries operate as a unified army against external threats. The chief "external threat" at the time was the Soviet Bloc of nations: the Soviet Union and countries it dominated in eastern Europe, China under its new Communist government, and North Korea.

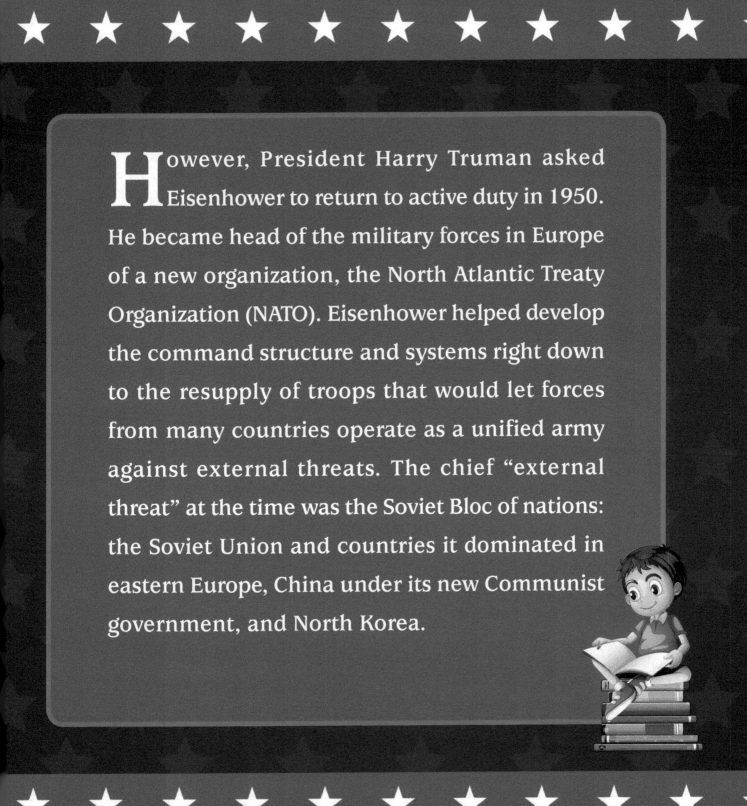

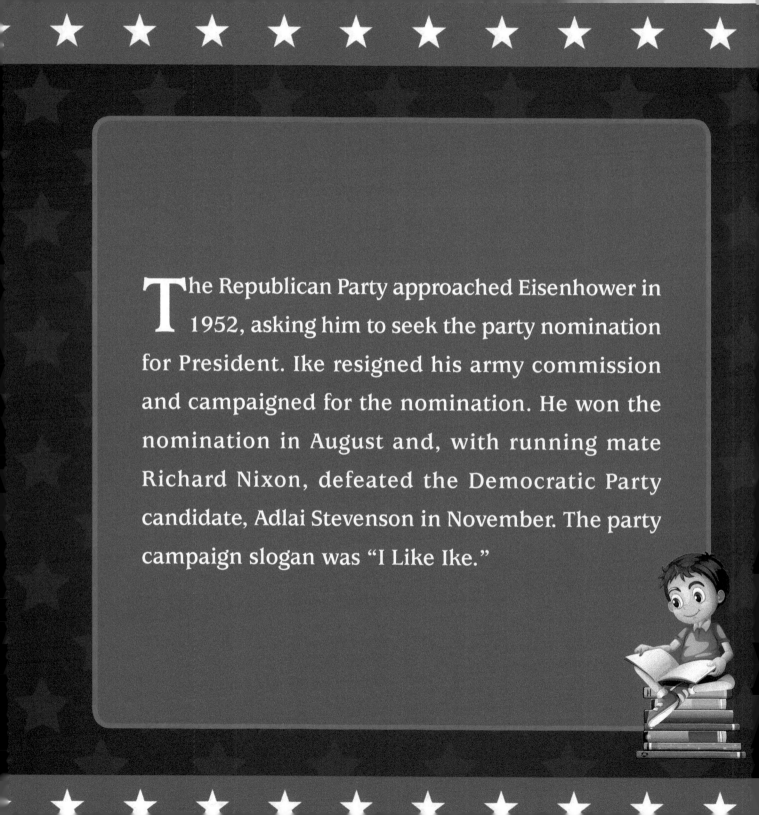

The Republican Party approached Eisenhower in 1952, asking him to seek the party nomination for President. Ike resigned his army commission and campaigned for the nomination. He won the nomination in August and, with running mate Richard Nixon, defeated the Democratic Party candidate, Adlai Stevenson in November. The party campaign slogan was "I Like Ike."

PRESIDENT DWIGHT D. EISENHOWER

PRESIDENT DWIGHT D. EISENHOWER

Eisenhower became the 34th President of the United States. In 1956 he won reelection by an even wider margin, serving eight years in all.

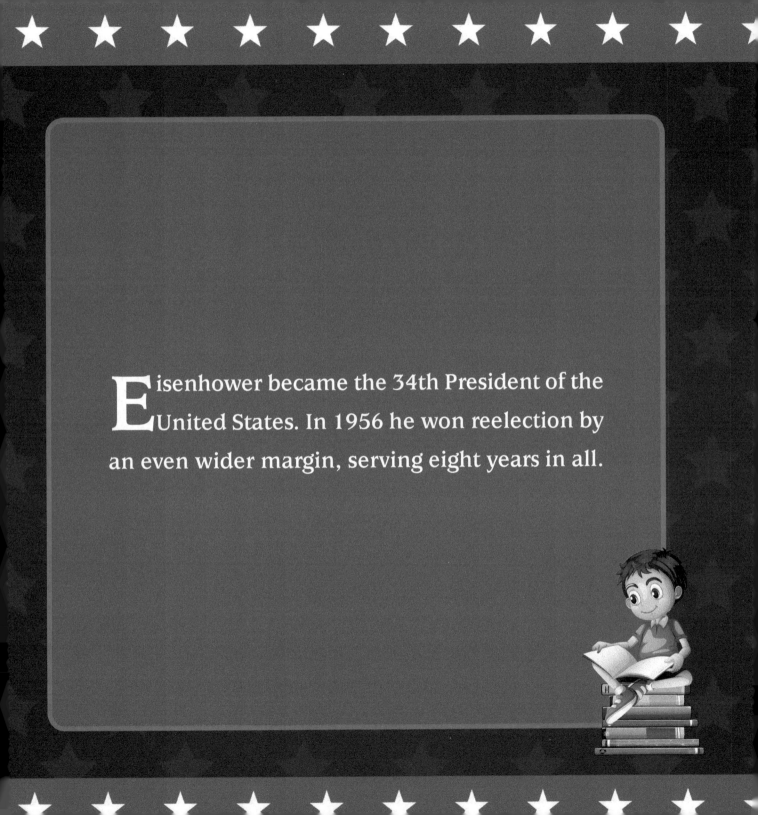

DOMESTIC POLICY

Although a Republican, Eisenhower found ways to work with the Democratic Party, which had a majority of votes in Congress for six of his eight years as president. The Eisenhower Administration continued programs that had been started by President Franklin Roosevelt (The New Deal) and President Truman (The Fair Deal).

PRESIDENT FRANKLIN ROOSEVELT

EISENHOWER EXECUTIVE OFFICE BUILDING

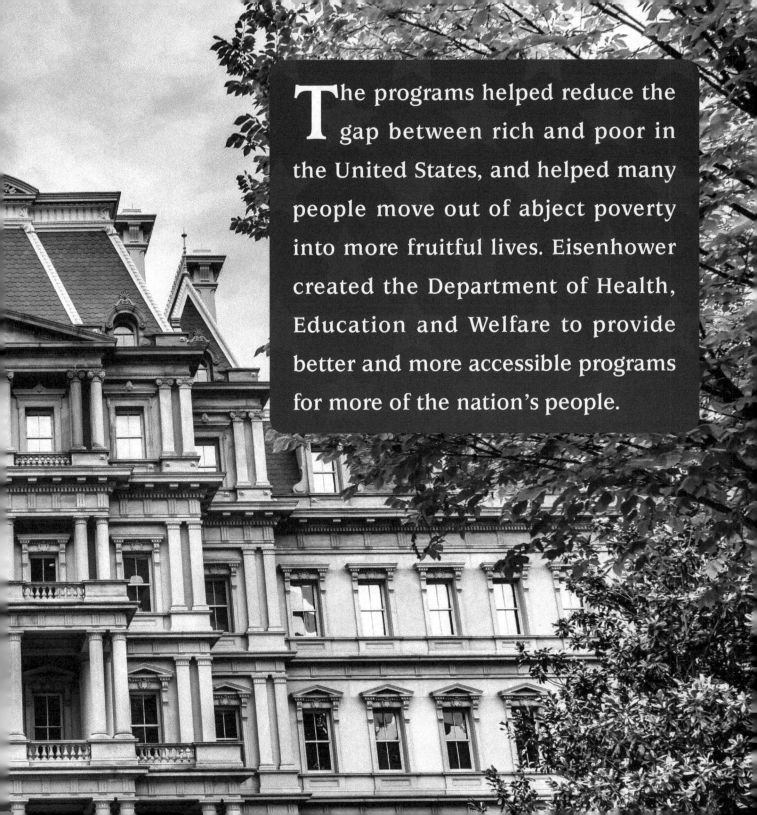

The programs helped reduce the gap between rich and poor in the United States, and helped many people move out of abject poverty into more fruitful lives. Eisenhower created the Department of Health, Education and Welfare to provide better and more accessible programs for more of the nation's people.

On another front, Eisenhower pushed for what became the Interstate Highway System. This program built over 40,000 miles of highways to connect the country from coast to coast and from the Mexican to the Canadian border. The highways made it possible to ship goods by truck more easily, and for people to travel farther from their home states for holidays and in search of work. The highways were also designed to make it easier for military forces to get to where they might be needed, in case the United States were ever invaded. This was the largest public-works project in United States history.

SUPREME COURT

Eisenhower was less effective in the struggle for racial equality. Although he enforced a 1954 Supreme Court decision ending the segregation of public schools, he did so slowly and reluctantly. He thought desegregation should not proceed too quickly and should wait until the white public was ready for it.

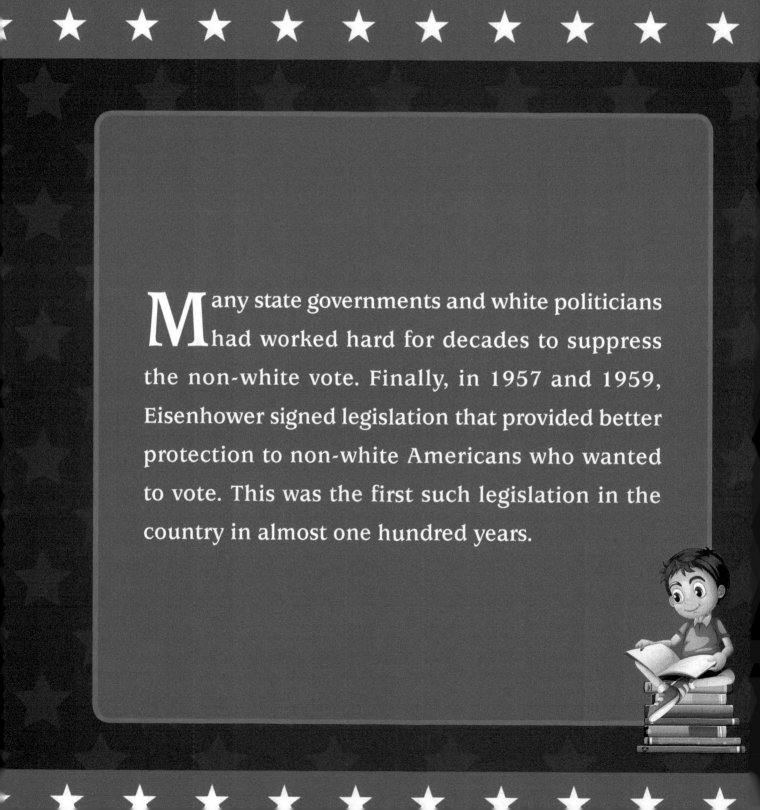

Many state governments and white politicians had worked hard for decades to suppress the non-white vote. Finally, in 1957 and 1959, Eisenhower signed legislation that provided better protection to non-white Americans who wanted to vote. This was the first such legislation in the country in almost one hundred years.

PRESIDENT DWIGHT D. EISENHOWER

EISENHOWER EXECUTIVE BUILDING

Another major issue in the United States under Eisenhower was the "red scare". This was a campaign of fear by anti-Communist groups, claiming that everything from the movie industry to the Federal Bureau of Investigation was infested with Communist spies. Because the leaders of the movement were Republican politicians and Eisenhower wanted to maintain party unity, he did not speak strongly against the hysteria and illegal tactics of the "red scare" campaign. He did, however, work behind the scenes to try to block the worst excesses of the movement.

FOREIGN POLICY

One of the first foreign policy acts of the Eisenhower administration in 1953 was signing an armistice bringing to an end the Korean War (1951-53). Ike did not use the force of the U.S. military often in international affairs, but he did authorized undercover actions against countries that supported the Soviet Union. Two of these programs overthrew democratically-elected governments in Iran (1953) and Guatemala (1954).

KOREAN WAR

In 1954, Ike declined to let the United States be drawn into the war between colonial French forces and the liberation movement in Vietnam. On the other hand, he supported the anti-communist government of South Vietnam, and this led to future U.S. involvement in the Vietnam War (1955-75).

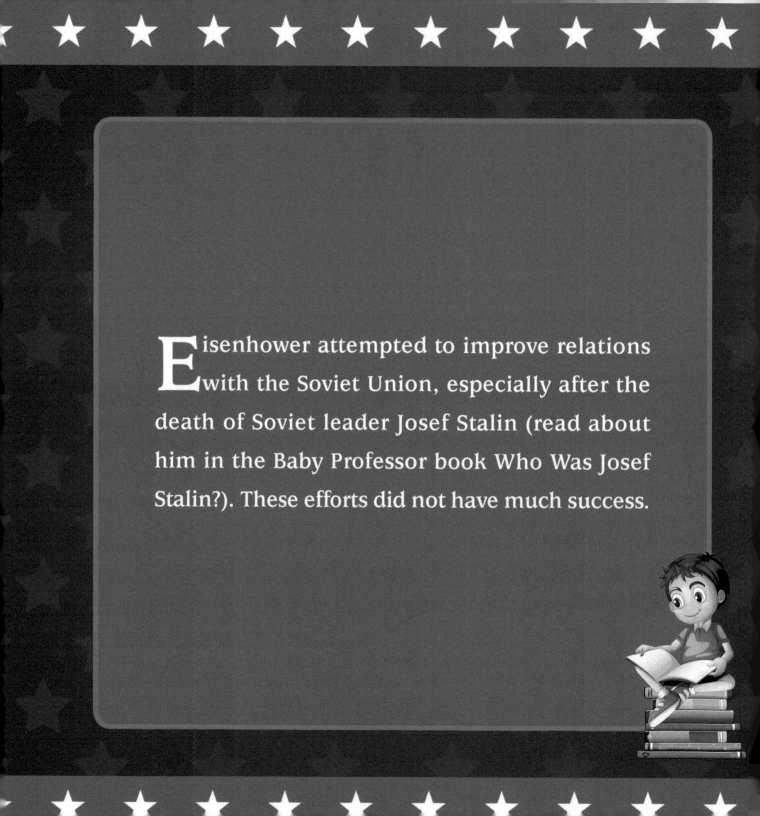

Eisenhower attempted to improve relations with the Soviet Union, especially after the death of Soviet leader Josef Stalin (read about him in the Baby Professor book Who Was Josef Stalin?). These efforts did not have much success.

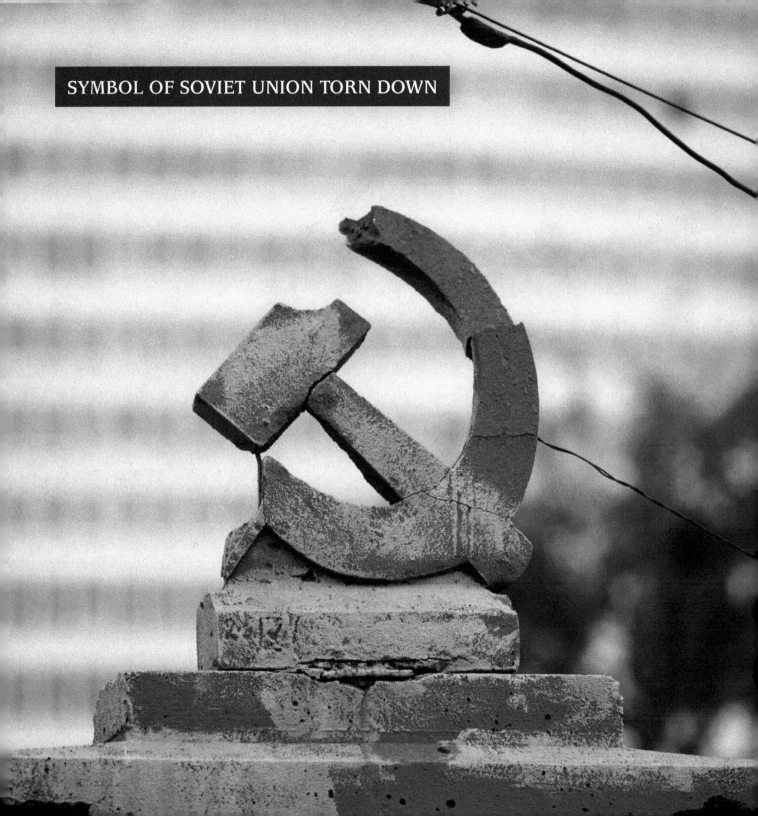

SYMBOL OF SOVIET UNION TORN DOWN

FINAL YEARS AND LEGACY

When he left office in 1961, Eisenhower spoke of the dangers to democracy of relying too much on the "military-industrial complex", where increased military spending and military activity are supported because it is good for the businesses building the guns and the bombs. Since tensions were still high between the west and the Soviet Bloc in what was called "the cold war", political leaders largely ignored Eisenhower's words.

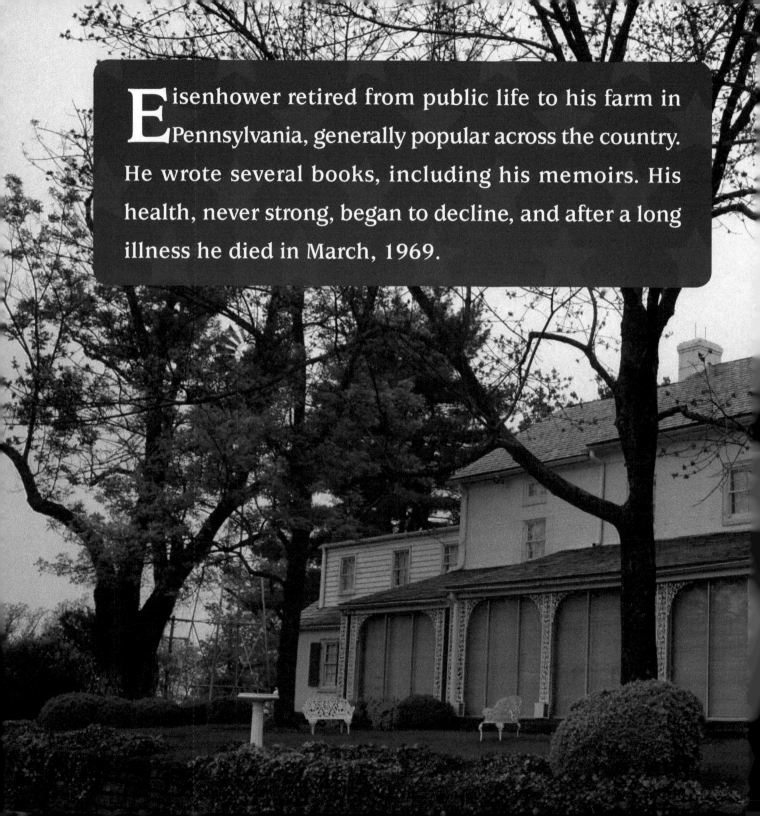

Eisenhower retired from public life to his farm in Pennsylvania, generally popular across the country. He wrote several books, including his memoirs. His health, never strong, began to decline, and after a long illness he died in March, 1969.

PRESIDENT DWIGHT EISENHOWER'S FARM

PRESIDENT DWIGHT EISENHOWER'S HOUSE

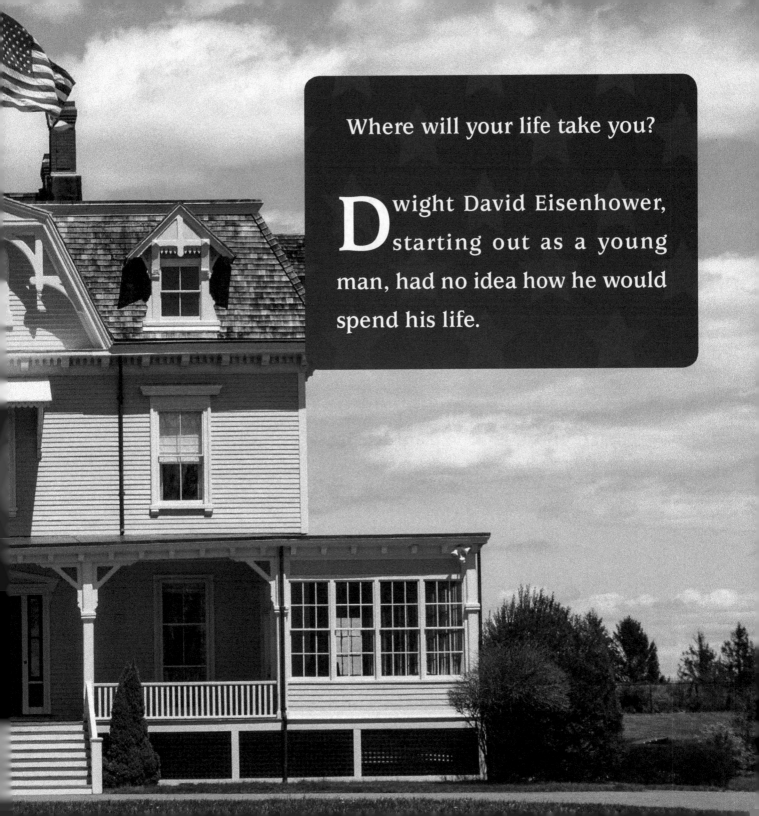

Where will your life take you?

Dwight David Eisenhower, starting out as a young man, had no idea how he would spend his life.

You can read about other people whose lives took unexpected turns in Baby Professor books like A Rich Man in Poor Man's Clothes: The Story of St. Francis of Assisi, Sally Ride: The First American Woman in Space, and Al Capone: A Dangerous Existence.

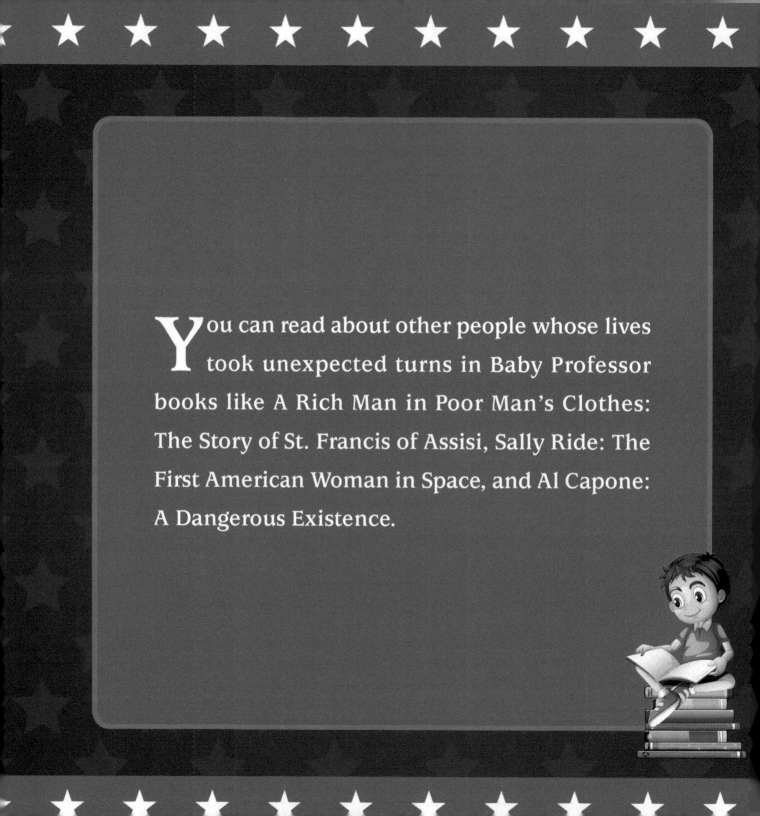

Visit

BABY PROFESSOR
EDUCATION KIDS

www.BabyProfessorBooks.com

to download Free Baby Professor eBooks
and view our catalog of new and exciting
Children's Books

Milton Keynes UK
Ingram Content Group UK Ltd.
UKHW050007300824
447530UK00002B/20